*A special thank you to illustrator Rachel Suzanne for adding some extra magic to this book. — E.C.*

The information contained in the book was deemed correct at the time of printing. While every effort has been made to check the veracity of the facts, the publisher will be happy to make any necessary corrections in future printings.

First published 2024 by Walker Books Ltd, 87 Vauxhall Walk, London SE11 5HJ

4 6 8 10 9 7 5 3

© 2024 Emily Coxhead

The right of Emily Coxhead to be identified as author of this work has been asserted in accordance with the Copyright, Designs and Patents Act 1988

EU Authorized Representative: HackettFlynn Ltd 36 Cloch Choirneal, Balrothery, Co. Dublin, K32 C942, Ireland EU@walkerpublishinggroup.com

This book has been typeset in HappyNews

Printed in Italy

All rights reserved. No part of this book may be reproduced, transmitted or stored in an information retrieval system in any form or by any means, graphic, electronic or mechanical, including photocopying, taping and recording, without prior written permission from the publisher.

Additionally, no part of this book may be used or reproduced in any manner for the purpose of training artificial intelligence technologies or systems, nor for text and data mining.

British Library Cataloguing in Publication Data: a catalogue record for this book is available from the British Library

ISBN 978-1-5295-2086-6

www.walker.co.uk

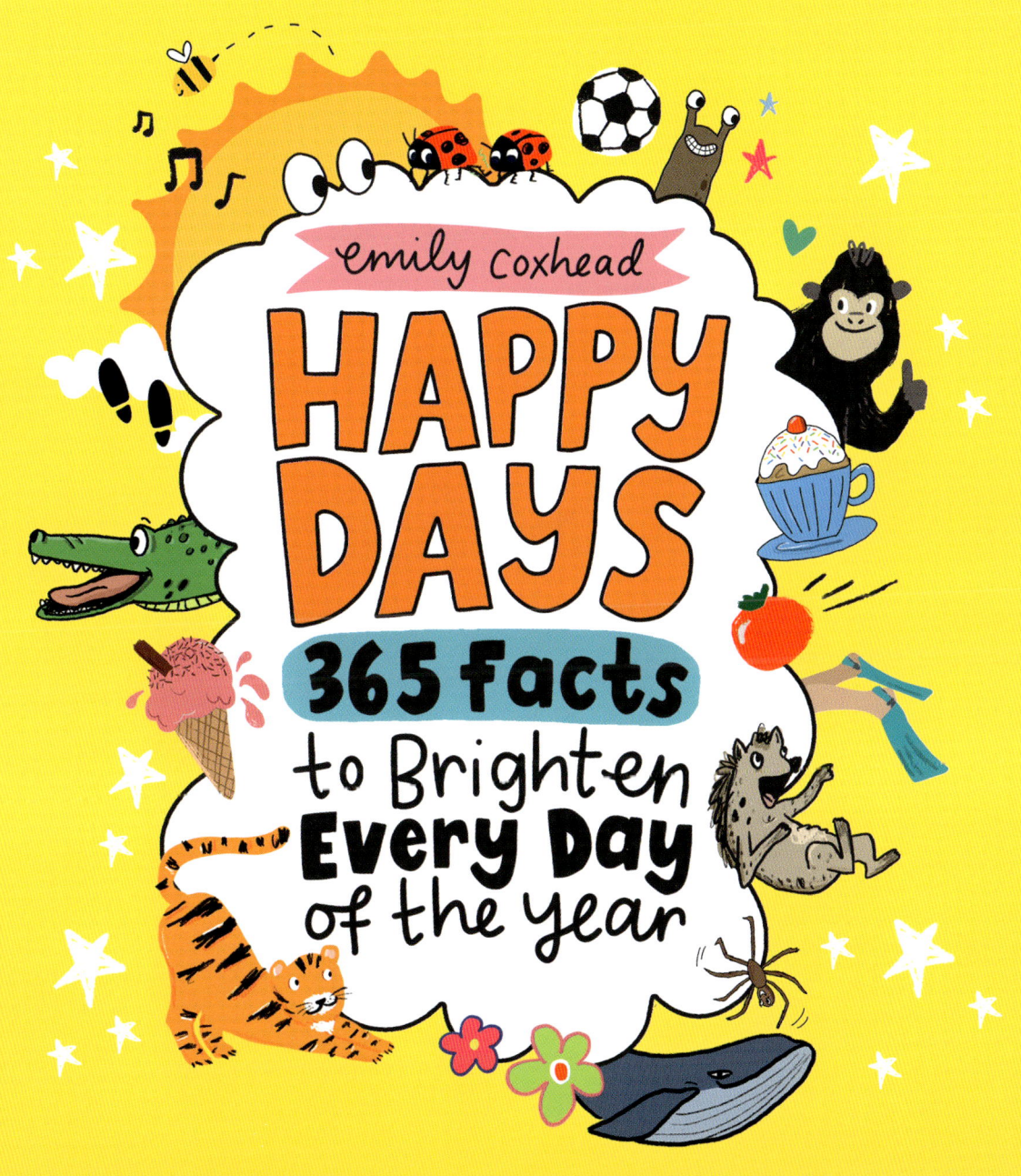

# January

**1st January**

When you smile, your body releases chemicals that will make you feel **HAPPIER**.

## 5th January

No two people see the **exact** same rainbow because of the way **light** reflects.

That means every rainbow is **UNIQUE** to you.

## 6th January

**One year** on Mercury is equal to about **88** Earth days. That means a 10-year-old on Earth would be **41 years** old on Mercury.

## 7th January

**Brno** in Czechia holds a **PARADE** of **silly walks** EVERY year.

8th January

The dinosaur with the LONGEST name is Micropachycephalosaurus.

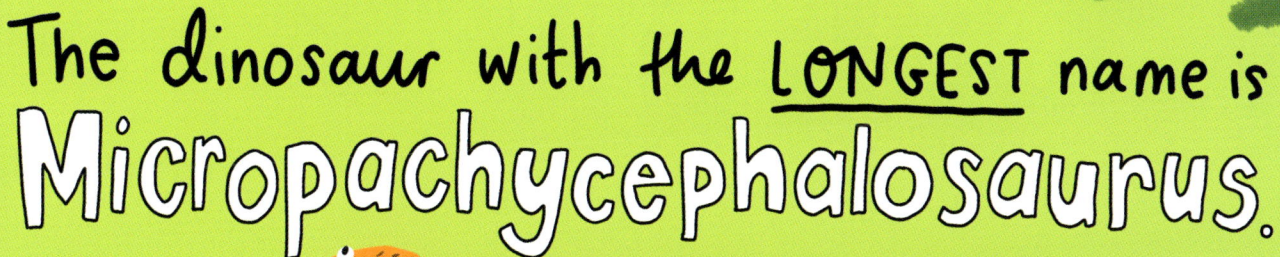

9th January

CUPCAKES got their name because they were first baked in ACTUAL cups.

**10th January**

# BANANAS

are curved because they grow towards the sun.

**11th January**

You can tell how OLD a tree is by the number of RINGS on its stump.

**12th January**

The Philippines has a word for the URGE to SQUEEZE cute things: gigil.

## 14th January

**ducks** SHAKE their tails when they're HAPPY.

## 15th January

A GROUP of PUGS is called a GRUMBLE.

16th January

A SCOTTISH musician created a WHOLE album of HAPPY SOUNDS.

17th January

Over 70 years after cheetahs were declared EXTINCT in INDIA, 4 cubs were born there.

### 18th January

# Hummingbirds

get their name from the `humming noise` their wings make because they beat *so fast*.

### 19th January

109-year-old Alfie Date, Australia's oldest man at the time, helped `injured` PENGUINS by knitting `tiny jumpers` for them.

### 20th January

The average person will spend about 79 days of their life brushing their teeth.

### 21st January

A GROUP of WEASELS is called a BOOGLE (or a confusion, or a sneak).

### 22nd January

Daisies close their petals at dusk and open them again at dawn, marking the beginning of a NEW day.

### 23rd January

The first-ever ORANGES were green.

24th January

# BRAILLE,

which helps blind people read through <u>touch</u>, was **invented** by 15-year-old Louis Braille, who lost his sight at the age of 3.

### 25th January

scotland has 421 words for snow, including feefle, snaw and skelf.

### 26th January

some buildings in HONG KONG have large holes in them designed for dragons to fly through.

**27th January**

An INDIAN company makes CRUNCHY SPOONS you can eat as an ALTERNATIVE to disposable spoons.

**28th January**

You can't hum if you hold your nose.

**29th January**

A BLUE WHALE'S tongue is heavier than an ELEPHANT.

**30th January**

One man's BLOOD donations saved more than 2 MILLION children's lives.

31st January

# A GROUP of GORILLAS is called a BAND (or a troop, or a whoop).

# February

**1st February**

The World's **LARGEST CUPCAKE** weighed over **1,000 kilograms** — that's about as heavy as **5** baby ELEPHANTS.

**2nd February**

A group of PENGUINS on land is called a WADDLE; on water it is called a RAFT.

**3rd February**

Astronauts have grown LETTUCE and CABBAGE in space without any soil.

**4th February**

The average person uses 57 sheets of toilet paper in 1 day.

**5th February**

According to the "World Sports Encyclopedia", there are more than 8,000 SPORTS played around the world.

**6th February**

The Great Barrier Reef in Australia is the LARGEST living structure on the planet. It can be seen from SPACE.

### 7th February

**GIRAFFE necks are very long** but they only have **7** bones in them – the same amount as **YOU.**

### 8th February

**Acacia trees** can warn each other of **DANGER.**

**9th February**

There are some species of mushroom that GLOW in the dark.

**10th February**

The highest-ever PANCAKE FLIP was a WHOPPING 9.47 metres high.

**11th February**

A 91-year-old man in the USA knitted hats for the homeless from his hospice bed.

**12th February**

GORILLAS BURP when they are HAPPY.

13th February

NIGHT RAINBOWS are a REAL thing. They are called MOONBOWS and only appear when the moon is VERY full and the sky is clear with no other light around.

14th February

OTTERS hold hands when they SLEEP so they don't float away from each other.

**15th February** — In Japan ORIGAMI PAPER CRANES are a symbol of PEACE and HOPE.

**16th February** — Buckingham Palace in London has 78 bathrooms.

### 17th February

**WELLY WANGING** is a sport where competitors throw a WELLINGTON BOOT as far as possible.

### 18th February

**BUTTERFLIES** taste plants with their feet.

### 19th February

There's a type of sea worm that has a pair of eyes on its Bum.

20th February

The **FIRST** pizza ever made was served to **QUEEN MARGHERITA** of Italy. It was topped with **WHITE** CHEESE, **GREEN** basil and **RED** tomatoes to match the colours of the Italian flag.

**23rd February**

LOOKING at photos of PUPPIES and KITTENS can HELP you concentrate.

**24th February**

A town in New Zealand built a (tunnel) under a busy road to help a group of BLUE PENGUINS travel safely to sea from their nesting area.

Penguin Crossing

25th February

# A GROUP of HYENAS is called a CACKLE.

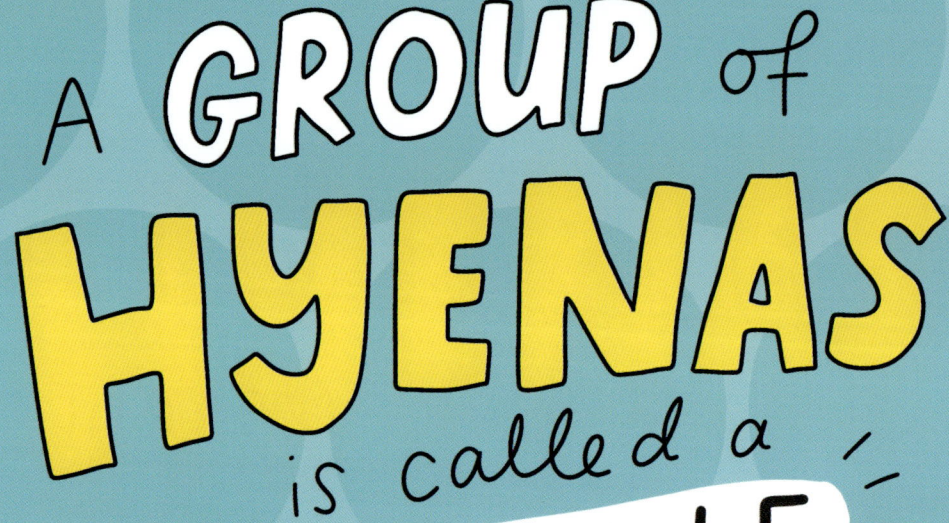

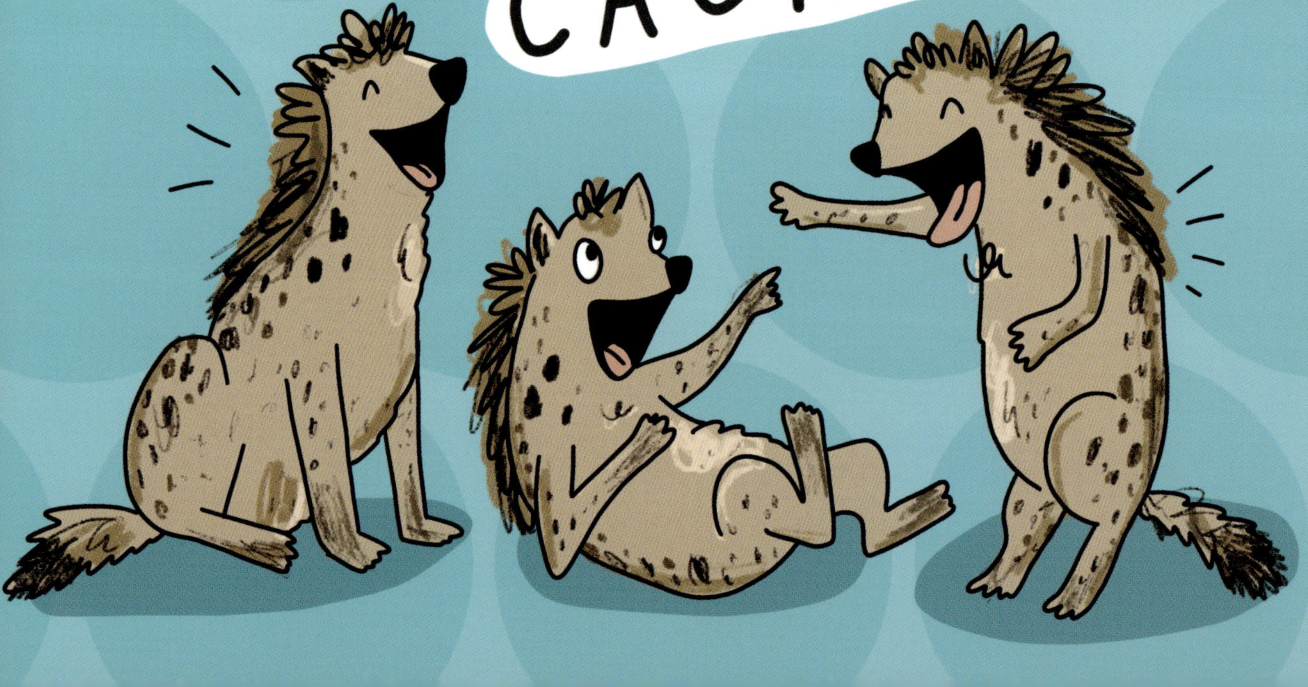

26th February

EVERY year in Italy they have a 3-day food fight called the BATTLE OF THE ORANGES, where people throw oranges at each other.

27th February

Some Vikings were buried with board games so they wouldn't be BORED in the afterlife.

28th February

Some flowers, such as NASTURTIUMS and VIOLAS, are edible.

# March

**1st March**

# Baby Elephants suck on their TRUNKS like human babies suck on their thumbs.

**2nd March**

One of Uranus's moons is called Margaret.

**3rd March**

A group of FROGS is called an ARMY.

**4th March**

On a single day in 2018 volunteers in India planted 66 million trees.

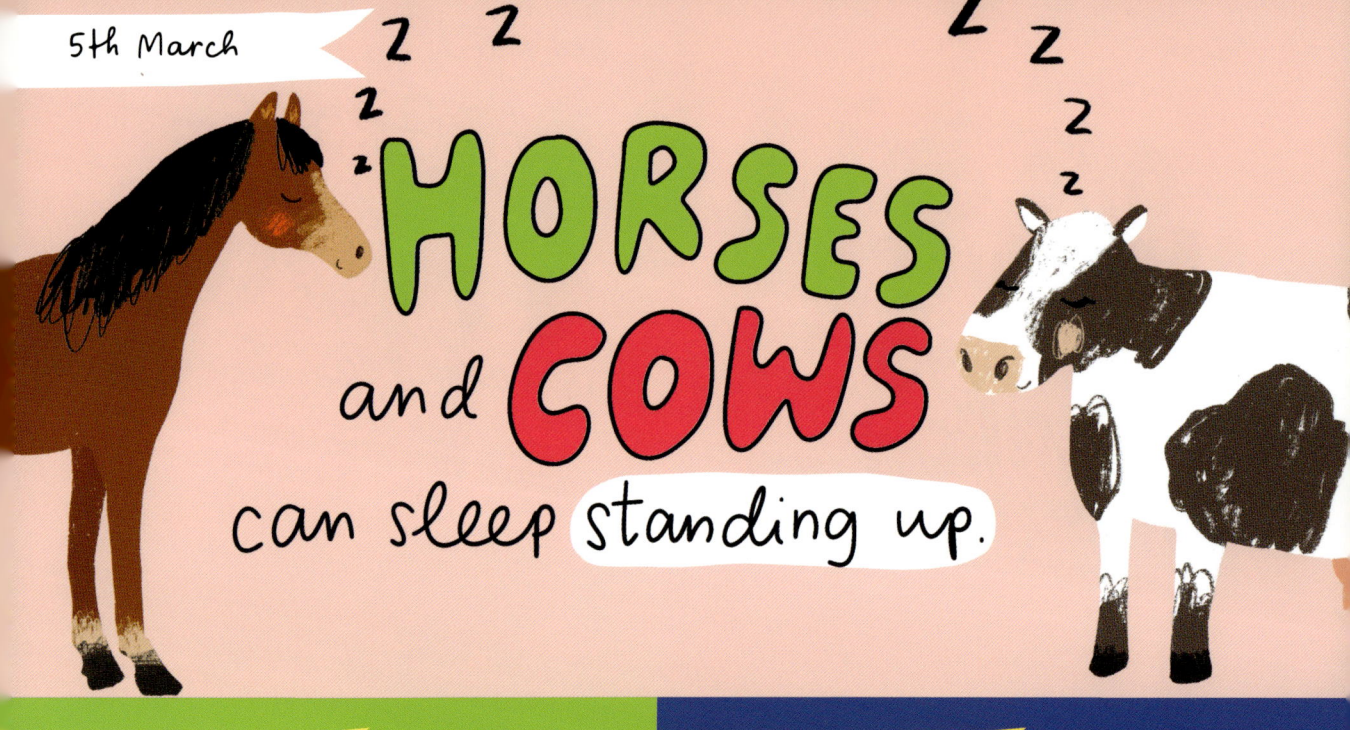

8th March

The FEAR of long words is called **hippopotomonstrosesquippedaliophobia**.

9th March

The world record for the LARGEST number of candles on a BIRTHDAY CAKE is 72,585.

### 10th March

In 2022 a person solved **6,931** Rubik's Cubes in 24 hours.

### 11th March

A group of **SHARKS** is called a shiver.

### 12th March

In Welsh mythology **FAIRIES** ride corgis into battle.

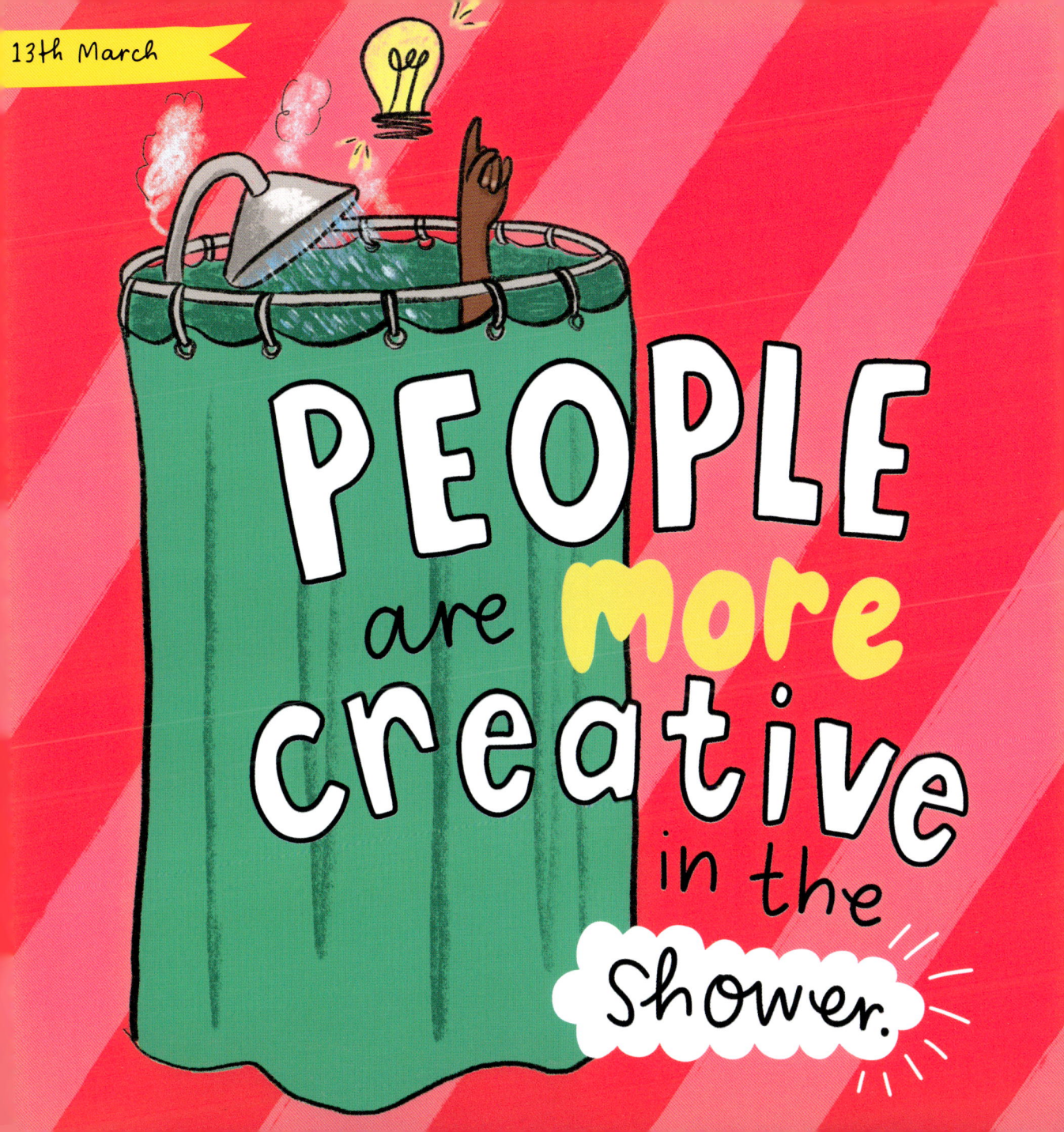

**14th March**

A cow in the USA gave birth to quadruplets; Eeny, meeny, miny and moo.

**15th March**

Orangutans and humans share about 97% of their DNA.

**16th March**

One of the **cutest** PLANTS on Earth is a succulent that has two furry "ears" like a **bunny**.

**17th March**

**EVERY** year **Chicago** in the USA dyes its river **GREEN** for St Patrick's Day.

**18th March**

Australia is WIDER than the MOON. The moon is 3,475 kilometres wide, while Australia is almost 4,000 kilometres wide.

**19th March**

Playing MUSIC to PLANTS helps them GROW FASTER.

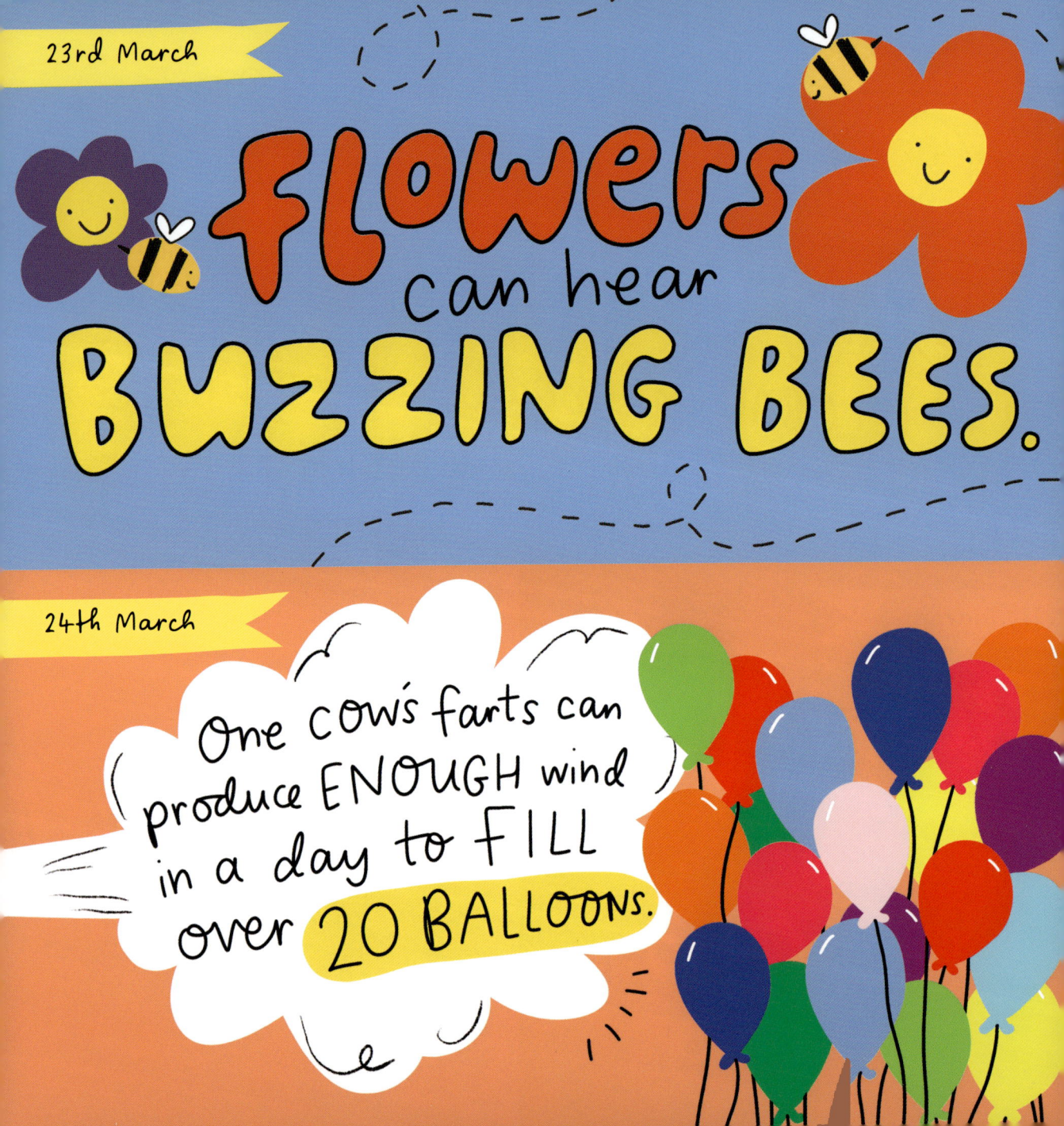

**25th March**

Some of Saturn's moons are shaped like pieces of ravioli.

**26th March**

New Zealand & Wales both have more sheep than humans.

**27th March**

People used to say "PRUNES" instead of "CHEESE" when being photographed.

**28th March**

HONEY never spoils because it's a natural bacteria killer.

**29th March**

your nose and ears continue growing your ENTIRE life.

**30th March**

Listening to and PLAYING music can help improve your memory.

## 2nd April

KETCHUP used to be SOLD as MEDICINE.

## 3rd April

Bats' chirps and SQUEAKS vary depending on where they live.

## 4th April

ASTRONAUTS WEAR SPECIAL NAPPIES on space walks that let them pee in their space suits.

5th April

SEA OTTERS use their tummies as plates when they eat.

6th April

In ancient Rome people sometimes used CROCODILE poo as make-up.

7th April

A blue whale's heartbeat is so LOUD that it can be detected 20 miles away.

8th April

# moon flowers BLOOM

when the moon is out.

9th April

# mother hens

can communicate with their chicks BEFORE they hatch.

CHEEP CHEEP!

10th April

ROSES are related to APPLES, PLUMS, CHERRIES, RASPBERRIES, PEARS and PEACHES.

11th April

The average person walks enough steps in their lifetime to take them around the world 3 times.

12th April

The FIRST meal eaten in space was beef and liver paste from SQUEEZY TUBES with chocolate sauce for dessert.

13th April

# GOATS BLEAT in different accents.

Bonjour

**14th April**

A GROUP of Puffins is called a CIRCUS

(or a gathering, or an improbability).

**15th April**

Giethoorn village in the Netherlands is car-free, which means you can ONLY travel on foot, by bicycle or by boat.

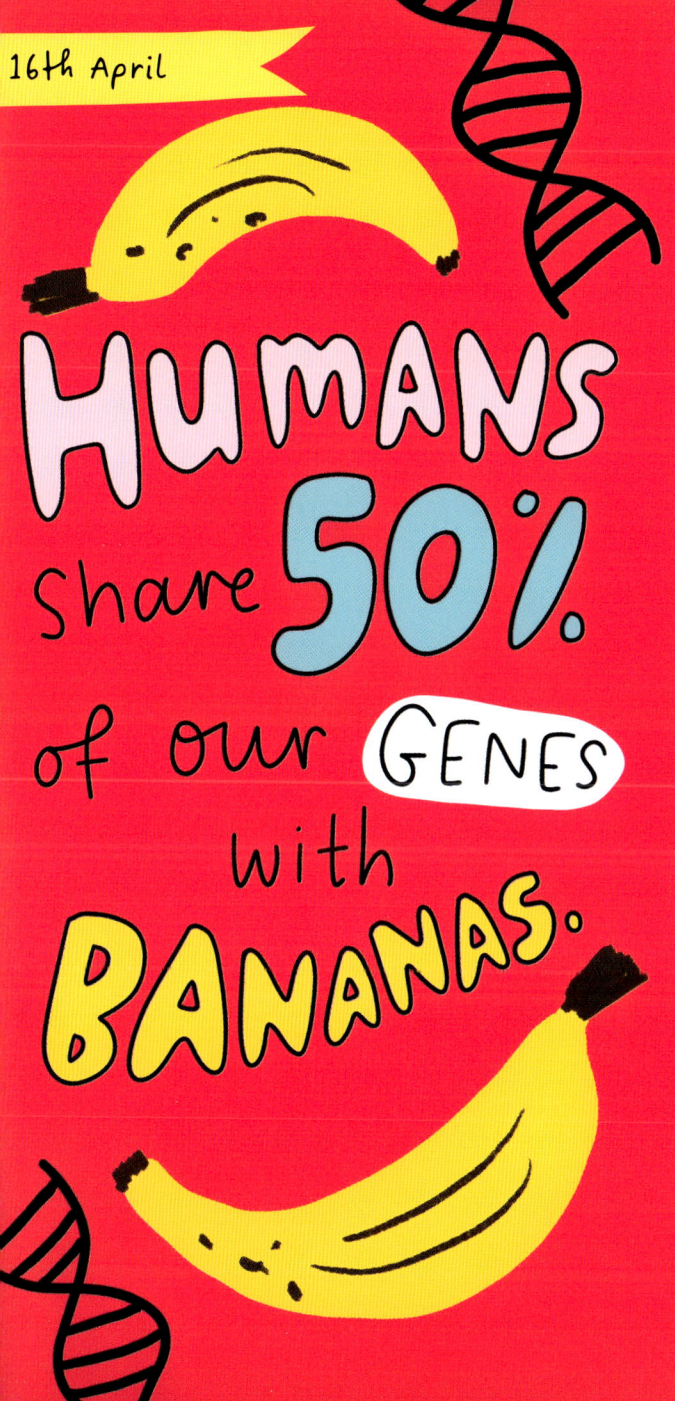

**16th April**

HUMANS share 50% of our GENES with BANANAS.

**17th April**

In Japan there is 1 vending machine for every 40 people.

Japanese vending machines sell a HUGE range of items, from ice cream and hot dogs to toilet paper and UMBRELLAS.

20th April

When RABBITS are HAPPY, they jump and twist around in a move called a BINKY.

21st April

The Water in Lake Hillier, Australia, is completely pink.

22nd April

The average person will sleep for 2,920 HOURS in a year — that's nearly 122 DAYS.

### 23rd April

**Zalipie** is a village in Poland where EVERY surface, including all the buildings, is painted with pictures of flowers.

### 24th April

## caterpillars have 12 eyes.

## 25th April

**Macaroni Penguins** mate for *life*.

## 26th April

Eating beans REALLY does make you fart. This is because they contain a type of CARBOHYDRATE that is difficult for your body to digest.

**27th April**

A 104-year-old woman in India recently learned to read for the FIRST time.

**28th April**

Cycle ball is a team sport which originated in Germany. It is like FOOTBALL but played on bikes.

**29th April**

A group of Jellyfish is called a Fluther (or a swarm, or a smack).

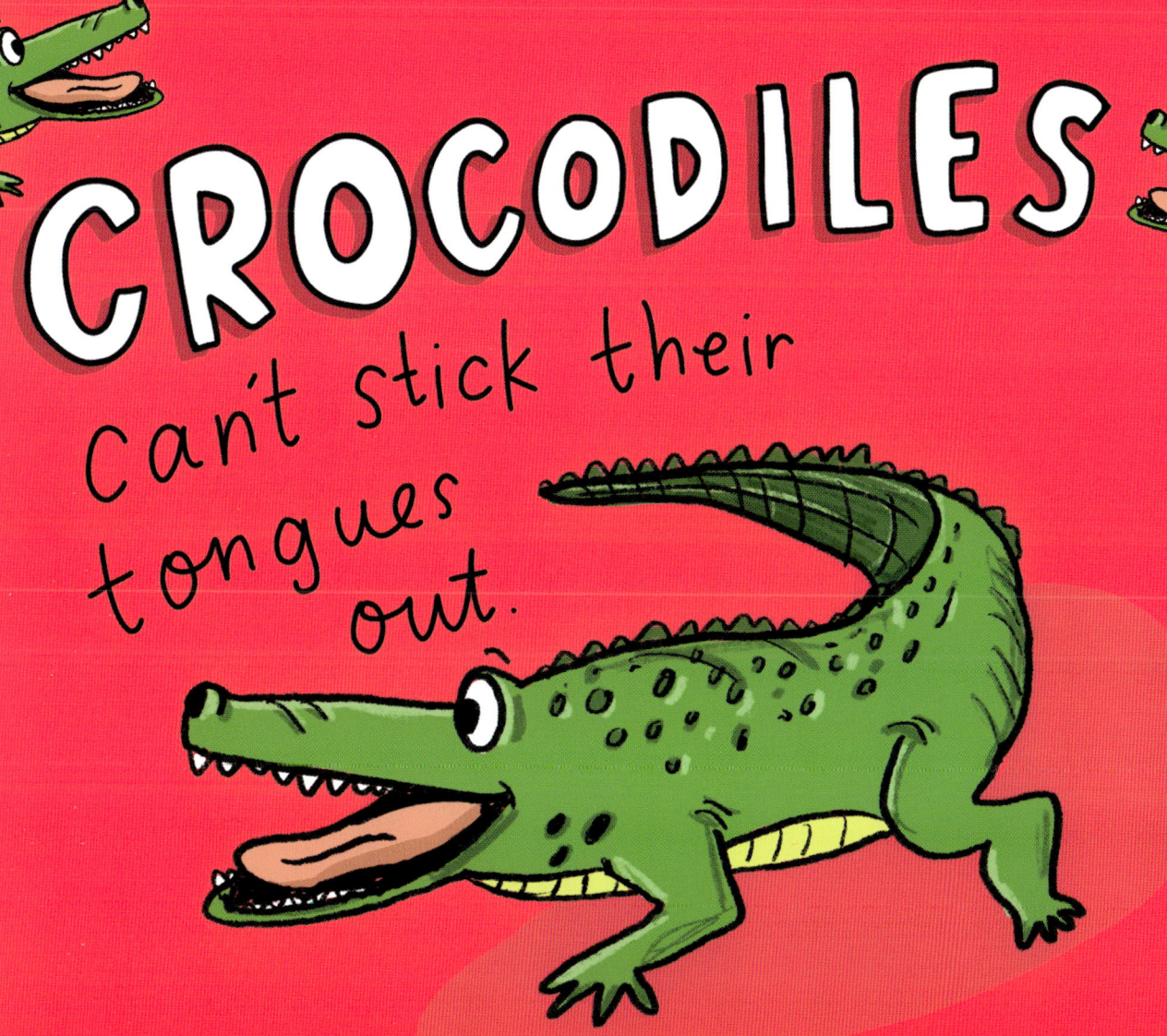

# May

**1st May**

The world's LARGEST bunch of BANANAS contained 473 individual pieces of fruit

— which is enough for over **2 years** worth of packed lunches.

**2nd May**

One day on the moon lasts ABOUT 27 Earth days.

**3rd May**

A GROUP of MICE is called a mischief.

**4th May**

There is a FOOTBALL club in Germany where the mascot is a REAL live goat called Hennes.

5th May — The Netherlands gifts 20,000 TULIPS to Canada EVERY year.

6th May — people grow nearly 1,000 kilometres of HAIR in their lifetime.

7th May — A HUMAN TONGUE is made up of 8 muscles.

8th May

A dog's NOSE PRINT is as UNIQUE as a human fingerprint.

9th May

For over 30 YEARS a group of American women known as the 9 NANAS secretly baked hundreds of CAKES to give away.

### 10th May

In Rwanda an organization called the **GORILLA GUARDIAN CLUB** pays for former poachers to **PROTECT** rare gorillas.

### 11th May

**FRESH AIR** is scientifically proven to give **you more energy.**

### 12th May

**EVERY** time a *baby girl* is born in the Indian village of Piplantri, the residents plant **111 TREES** in her honour.

14th May

There are **MOUNTAINS** and **VOLCANOES** in the **OCEAN**.

15th May

**GIRAFFE** populations across many African countries have **INCREASED** due to massive **CONSERVATION** efforts.

16th May

The Inuit word iktsuarpok means "the feeling you get when you are waiting for a visitor to ARRIVE and keep looking out to check if they are coming yet".

17th May

The TRADITION of SHAKING HANDS began as a way of showing that you weren't holding a WEAPON.

18th May

SEA LIONS are the ONLY animals that can CLAP to a beat.

19th May

A GROUP of PORCUPINES is called a PRICKLE.

### 20th May

A road in London is closed for **3 WEEKS** EVERY year to allow **TOADS** to cross during breeding season.

### 21st May

The **OLDEST** musical instrument in the world is the **NEANDERTHAL FLUTE**, which is over 50,000 years old.

### 22nd May

**Italy** holds an ANNUAL **HIDE-AND-SEEK** world championship.

23rd May

HIPPOS who live in the Mara river, KENYA, dump nearly 400 kilograms of POO into the water every day, helping to keep the river healthy.

24th May

Originally CARROTS were PURPLE and YELLOW NOT orange!

### 25th May

The number of **TIGERS** is increasing, which is **GREAT NEWS** for the **ENDANGERED** species.

### 26th May

At an annual **CHEESE-ROLLING** competition in Gloucestershire, UK, hundreds of people race downhill to catch a wheel of **CHEESE!**

### 27th May
It can take **7 to 21 days** to make a single **JELLY BEAN**.

### 28th May
Birds even sing in their **DREAMS**.

### 29th May
In 2015 a Canadian **ASTRONAUT** released an album of SONGS that he had recorded on the International Space Station.

### 30th May
**TEA** is the second most widely consumed drink in the world after water.

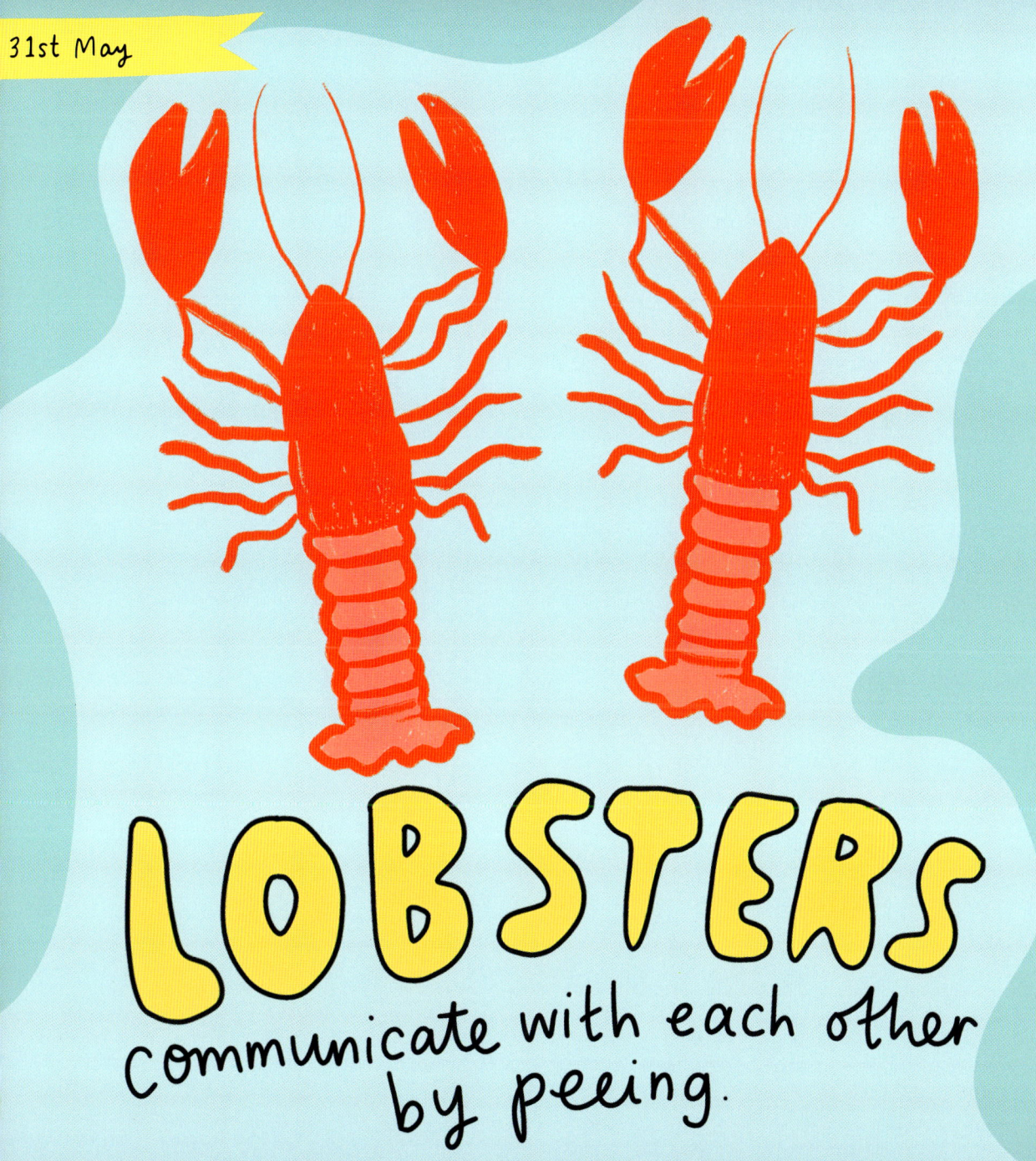

**2nd June**

EVERY household in Wales has been given a FREE tree to plant to help tackle CLIMATE CHANGE.

**3rd June**

SLUG blood is GREEN.

**4th June**

BABY turtles communicate with each other BEFORE they hatch.

**5th June**

TENNIS balls used to be WHITE but were changed to YELLOW to make them more visible for television viewers.

**6th June**

The first recorded time that STRAWBERRIES and CREAM were served together were at a royal banquet in 1509.

**7th June**

Spinner DOLPHIN POO can help save coral reefs by providing them with vital nitrogen.

8th June

In Leicester, UK, some **bus stops** have **roof gardens** to help pollinators such as **bees**.

9th June

LADYBIRDS smell with their feet.

**10th June**

A hotel made ENTIRELY out of SAND was once built in Weymouth, U.K.

**11th June**

PIGEONS can be taught to recognize words.

**12th June**

A toy pirate ship travelled 6,000 kilometres across the Atlantic Ocean.

13th June

A GROUP of ladybirds is called a LOVELINESS.

14th June

# PUPPIES can be BORN as IDENTICAL TWINS.

15th June

# The OLDEST operating ROLLER COASTER
in the world was built in 1902 and is made of wood.

**16th June**

# Lemons float, but Limes sink.

**17th June**

A preschool in **JAPAN** has a courtyard that's designed to collect rain water into a giant **PUDDLE** so children can play in it.

## 18th June

# MUMMY DOLPHINS
"sing" to their babies in the womb.

## 19th June

A rubbish collector in Colombia built a FREE library out of 20,000 BOOKS found in bins.

**20th June**

A man in South Africa soared for a distance of **15 miles** attached to **100 helium balloons.**

**21st June**

The world record for the longest chain of people licking lollipops is 12,831.

**22nd June**

**SLUGS** have approximately **27,000** TEETH! That's more than a shark.

23rd June

# GENTOO PENGUINS

spend time finding a pebble to give to their mate in order to PROPOSE.

24th June

# A GROUP of SLOTHS is called a SNUGGLE.

25th June

**FORESTS in Scotland are the LARGEST** they have been for 900 years!

26th June

The Argentinian footballer **messi** once scored **91 GOALS** in a year in professional games, setting a NEW world record.

**27th June**

In a city in Massachusetts, USA, many residents learned sign language so that they could communicate with a deaf girl in their neighbourhood.

**28th June**

EVERYONE'S TONGUE print is as UNIQUE as their FINGERPRINTS.

**29th June**

Orangutans blow raspberries at each other as they go to SLEEP.

**2nd July**

APPLES give you more ENERGY than coffee does.

**3rd July**

The longest-ever marriage lasted 86 years and 290 days.

**4th July**

Yuma, a city in Arizona, USA, is the sunniest place on Earth, where the sun shines at least 91% of the year.

**5th July**

Woodpeckers have VERY long tongues — a third of their body length.

**6th July**

Being near bodies of water, such as SEAS, OCEANS, lakes & rivers, can make you HAPPIER.

**7th July**

A RAINBOW in Taiwan lasted a RECORD-BREAKING 8 hours and 58 minutes.

**8th July**

Each of the **5 Olympic rings** is a DIFFERENT COLOUR to represent the **5 parts of the world** — a symbol of international TOGETHERNESS.

**9th July**

COWS LICK each other as a sign of FRIENDSHIP.

### 10th July

The **most** remote inhabited island on Earth — Tristan da Cunha — is over 2,000 kilometres from its nearest neighbour, South Africa.

### 11th July

Baby Otters are VERY fluffy when they're born, which helps them swim.

### 12th July

Hawaiian PIZZA was actually invented in Canada.

13th July

A group of **BUTTERFLIES** is called a *kaleidoscope.*

## 14th July

A **spotted skunk** will do a HANDSTAND to intimidate predators.

## 15th July

The dot on top of an "i or j" is called a tittle.

**16th July**

# SUNSHINE & WARMTH
*make you friendlier.*

**17th July**

The furthest a **PAPER PLANE** has travelled when thrown is **69.14 metres**.

**18th July**

A BRITISH company makes SWIMWEAR ENTIRELY out of RECYCLED plastic waste.

**19th July**

COWS HAVE BEST FRIENDS.

### 20th July

A GROUP of STARFISH is called a galaxy.

### 21st July

A former Royal Marine was the FIRST blind person to successfully row all the way across the Pacific Ocean.

### 22nd July

At the 2020 Tokyo Olympics the medals were made of metal that had been recycled from donated electronic devices.

**23rd July**

Zebras fart LOUDLY with EVERY stride when they are being chased by Lions.

**24th July**

It's possible that footprints on the moon will still be there in 100 million years!

**25th July**

The world record for the most people licking ice cream at a single event is 2,728.

**26th July**

Some LADYBIRDS have STRIPES instead of SPOTS.

27th July

A **garden** snail can have up to **14,000** teeth.

28th July

Italy's oldest-EVER graduate gained his degree at **96** years old.

29th July

Those who are HAPPIEST tend to live a lot longer than those who are not.

30th July

Medals at the 2016 Paralympics contained steel balls so they could be heard by visually impaired medallists.

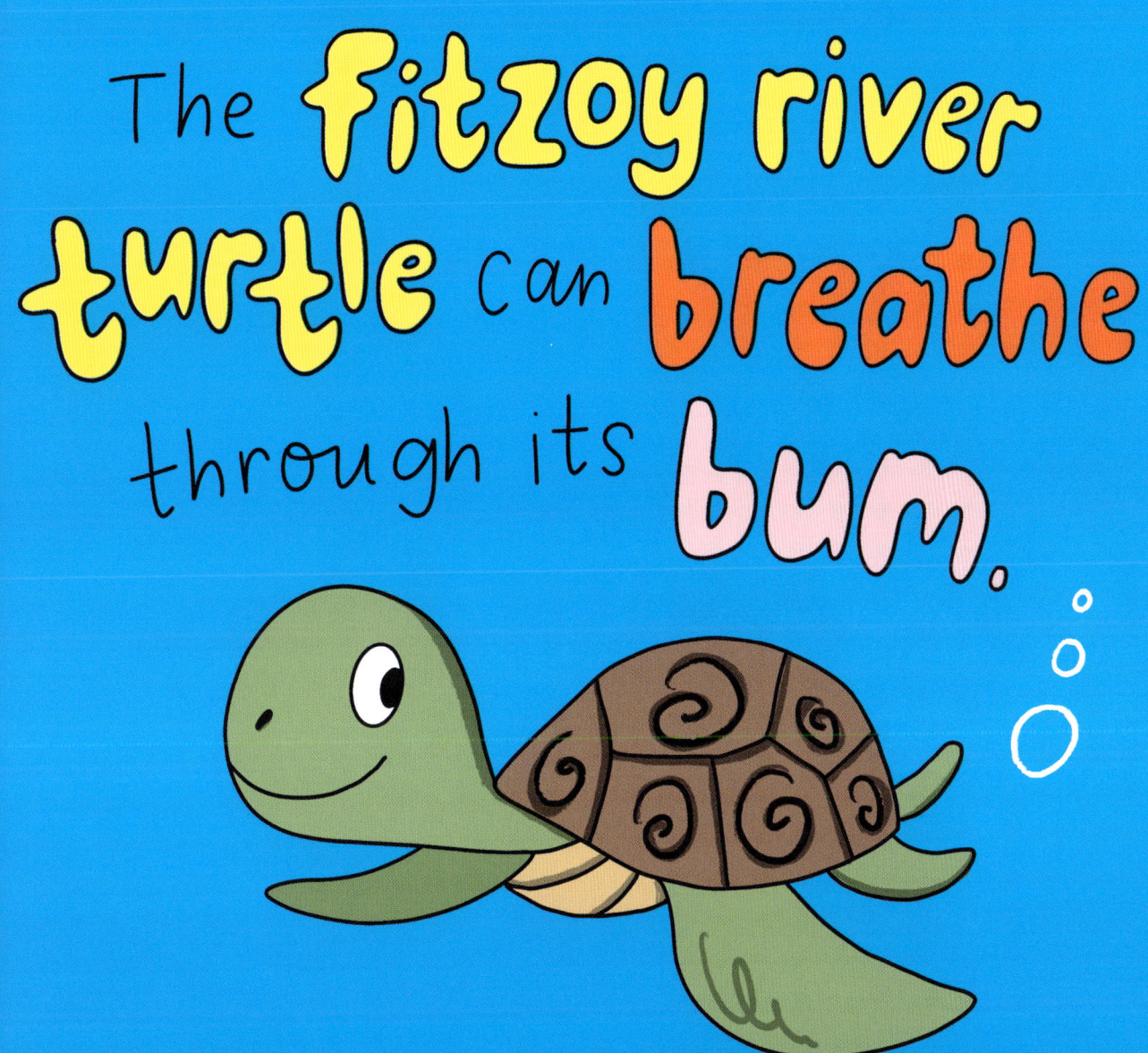

# August

**1st August**

It takes about **50 LICKS** to FINISH 1 scoop of ice cream.

**2nd August**

BROCCOLI is ACTUALLY a type of FLOWER.

**3rd August**

The longest-ever TENNIS MATCH lasted 11 hours and 5 minutes.

**4th August**

Only about 5% of the world's oceans have been explored.

**5th August**

ELEPHANTS can HEAR BETTER with one foot off the GROUND.

**6th August**

Mount Augustus in Australia is so ENORMOUS that it takes more than half an hour to drive around it.

**7th August**

PEANUT BUTTER gets stickier when you put it in your mouth.

**8th August**

# The world's *longest* sausage

measured 62.75 kilometres long.

**9th August**

# Octopuses collect SHINY THINGS and make gardens out of them.

### 10th August

Having a **HOUSEPLANT** can improve the **AIR QUALITY** in a room as well as reduce **STRESS** and **ANXIETY**.

### 11th August

**Pirates** thought that wearing earrings helped prevent **SEASICKNESS**.

### 12th August

**BABIES SLEEP** for an average of 5,400 **HOURS** in their first year of life.

13th August

# sunflowers

turn their heads throughout the day to follow the movement of the sun from east to west.

**14th August**

# KANGAROOS can't walk BACKWARDS.

**15th August**

# The average STRAWBERRY has 200 seeds.

**16th August**

Owning a pet can reduce anxiety and improve your social skills.

**17th August**

Even though **STEGOSAURUS** was a **HUGE** dinosaur, its brain was the size of a plum.

18th August

CHIMPANZEES can be TAUGHT how to play ROCK, PAPER, SCISSORS.

19th August

An old-fashioned name for a BUMBLEBEE is a "DUMBLEDORE."

20th August

# The Taj Mahal's DOME is held together with SUGAR, FRUIT JUICE and EGG whites!

21st August

# ICE LOLLIES were invented by an 11-year-old who accidentally left a stick in his drink on a cold evening.

22nd August

# The TOUCH-ME-NOT PLANT folds up its leaves when *touched.*

### 23rd August

EVERY GIRAFFE'S coat is UNIQUE, just like a HUMAN'S fingerprint.

### 24th August

A cat named Stubbs was elected HONORARY mayor of a town in Alaska, USA.

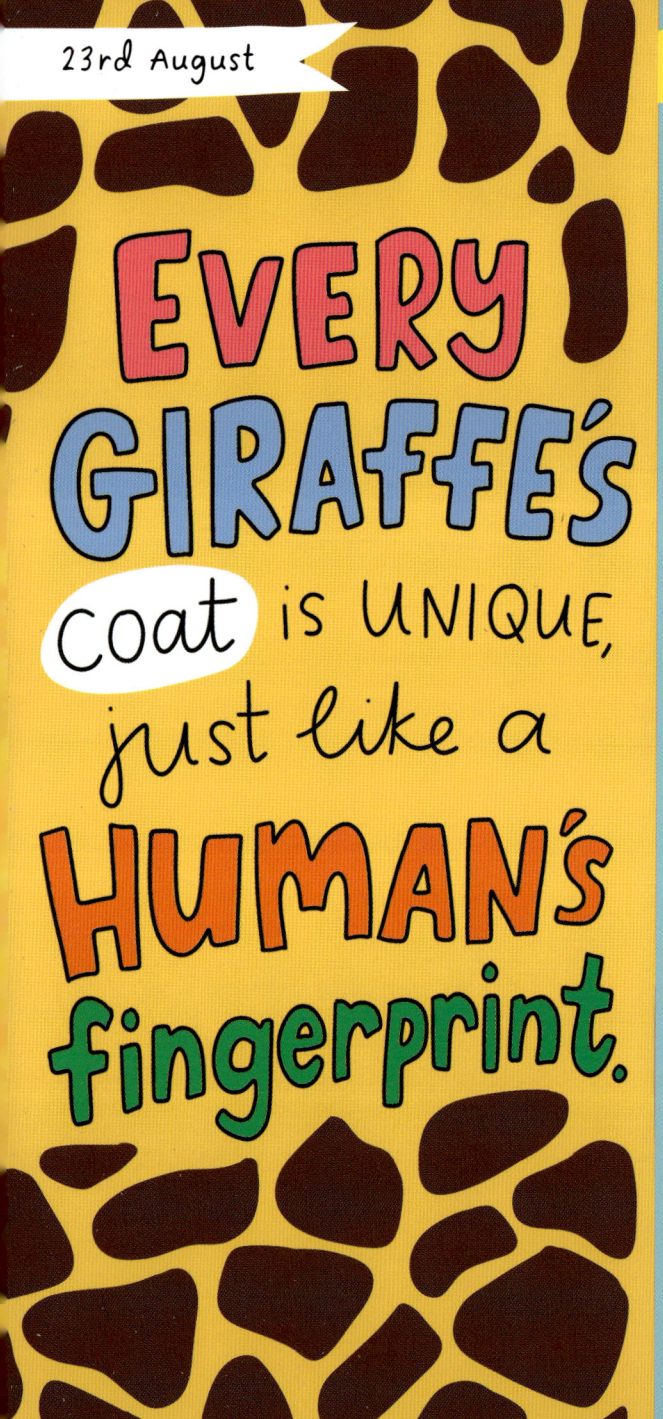

**25th August**

Every summer, Wales hosts the **World Bog Snorkelling Championships**, where competitors race through a bog in FLIPPERS and a SNORKEL.

**26th August**

During a street festival in Spain called La Tomatina, thousands of people hurl more than 100 tonnes of tomatoes at each other.

**27th August**

OLYMPIC GOLD MEDALS are mostly made of silver — with tiny bits of GOLD.

**28th August**

The oldest known work of ART (from 44,000 years ago) was recently discovered on an Indonesian island.

**29th August**

If a GECKO loses its tail, it can GROW ANOTHER ONE.

**30th August**

A man from Dorset, UK, holds the world record for the most JOKES told in 1 minute: 26!!

31st August

A GROUP of ELEPHANTS is called a PARADE. (or a herd).

TOOT TOOT

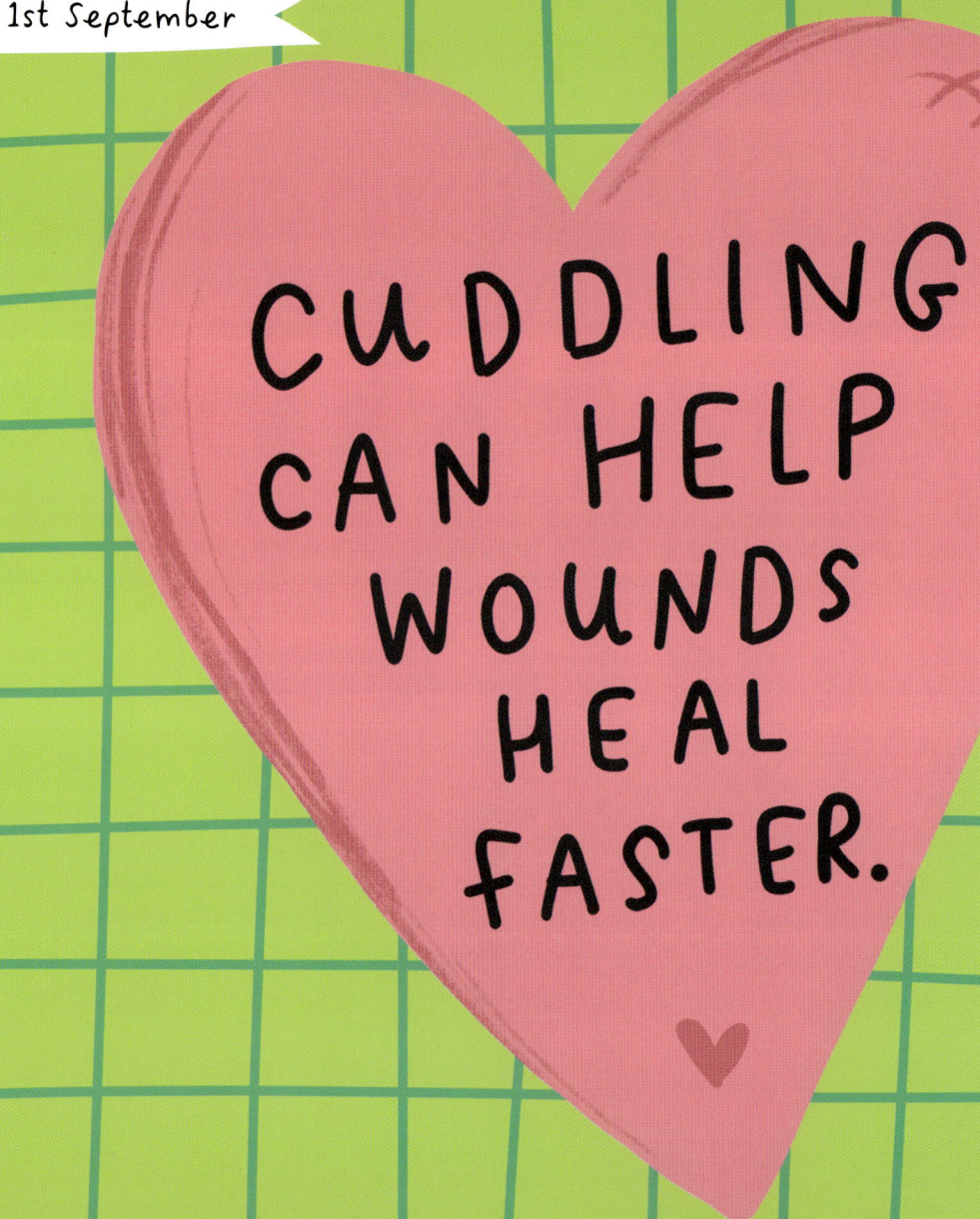

### 5th September

Pigeons were used to carry IMPORTANT messages during the World Wars. 32 pigeons were awarded medals for their BRAVERY.

### 6th September

There is a basketball court at the TOP of the US Supreme Court building.

### 7th September

Babies can LAUGH and SMILE before they can speak.

8th September

A shrimp's HEART is located in its HEAD.

9th September

TUG OF WAR used to be an Olympic sport.

### 10th September

A HEDGEHOG has over 5,000 PRICKLES.

### 11th September

Extreme ironing is a sport which involves IRONING items in remote locations. The first Extreme Ironing World Championships were held in 2002.

### 12th September

Goat moth caterpillars smell like GOATS.

13th September

An astronaut on the Apollo 17 mission wrote his daughter's initials on the moon.

**14th September**

Australia's HUMPBACK WHALE populations have increased so much they are no longer a threatened species.

**15th September**

The world's SMALLEST DOG is a chihuahua named PEARL who could fit in the palm of your hand.

16th September

The WORLD'S OLDEST tortoise is 190 years old... and counting!

17th September

Quokkas are known as the world's HAPPIEST animals because they are ALWAYS smiling.

18th September

WORMS communicate by CUDDLING each other.

19th September

Over 3 million species of PLANTS and ANIMALS call the Amazon Rainforest home.

**20th September**

SQUIRRELS will ADOPT other squirrel BABIES.

**21st September**

On average, a GOLF BALL has 336 dimples.

**22nd September**

In 2016 the UK public voted to name a polar research ship BOATY McBoatface.

**23rd September**

The world now has 2 permanent MUSEUMS focusing on how to be HAPPY: the Museum of Happiness in the UK and the Happiness Museum in DENMARK.

**24th September**

The OLDEST living tree in the world is over 4,800 years old, which is even older than the PYRAMIDS.

### 25th September

HORSES can remember if you SMILED the last time they saw you.

### 26th September

The OLDEST known case of DANDRUFF was found in the fossils of a dinosaur that lived 125 million years ago.

**27th September**

The Dead Sea in the Middle East is SO SALTY that you cannot sink in it.

**28th September**

The human THIGH BONE is stronger than CONCRETE.

**29th September**

A group of GOLDFINCHES is called a CHARM.

30th September

Rats are TICKLISH and even LAUGH when they're tickled.

"ha" "ha" "ha!"

# October

1st October

EVERY year thousands of NEW trees GROW because SQUIRRELS forget where they buried their nuts.

### 2nd October

The water that spills over the Niagara falls waterfall in 1 minute would fill multiple OLYMPIC-SIZED swimming pools.

### 3rd October

Sweden has 267,570 ISLANDS - the most of ANY country in the world.

### 4th October

Baby Koalas are the size of a 2 pence coin when they're born.

8th October

In the UK, **BICYCLE LIBRARIES** allow you to borrow bikes for **FREE**.

9th October

A **GROUP** of **Lemurs** is called a **conspiracy**.

### 10th October

Seahorses CHOOSE a mate for LIFE.

### 11th October

The Mariana Trench under the Pacific Ocean is DEEPER than Mount Everest is tall.

### 12th October

The FIRST movie ever made – The Horse in Motion (1878) – shows just a few seconds of a man riding a race horse.

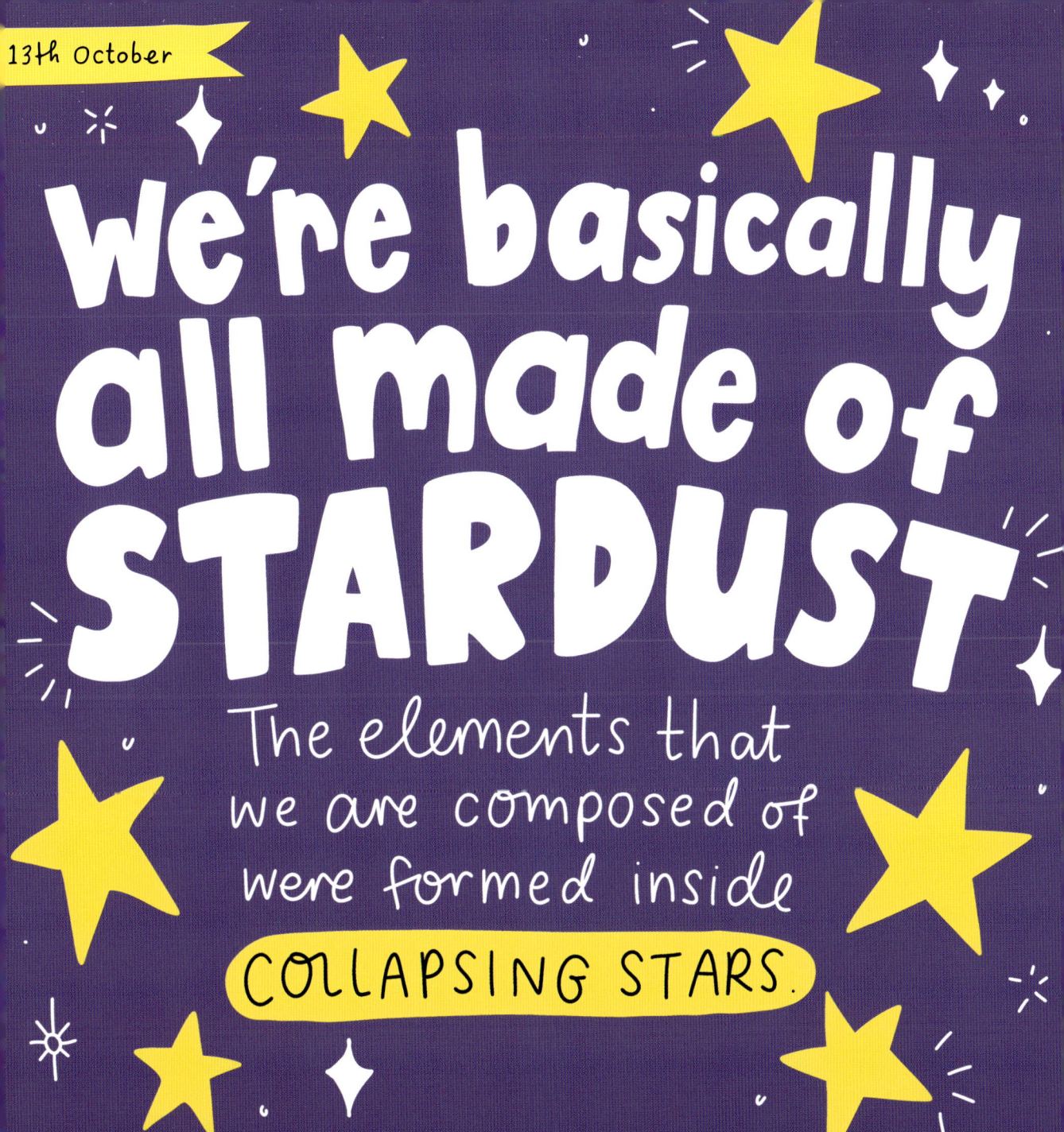

**14th October**

A **baby** hedgehog is called a **HOGLET**.

**15th October**

It takes more muscles to **FROWN** than it does to **SMILE**.

### 16th October

# The Vampire SQUID

avoids predators by turning itself inside out and wrapping its spiky bottom half over its body.

### 17th October

A **GROUP** of flamingos is called a FLAMBOYANCE.

18th October

A **Pangolin's tongue** is LONGER than its body.

19th October

The little BLOB of TOOTHPASTE on your brush is called a NURDLE.

20th October

Baby Sloths LOVE cuddling.

21st October

SAINT LUCIA is the ONLY country in the world named after a woman.

22nd October

A Dutch supermarket chain has SLOWER checkouts for lonely people who would like to chat.

**23rd October**

A GROUP of RABBITS is called a FLUFFLE.

**24th October**

One man single-handedly REPOPULATED a RARE butterfly species, called the California pipevine swallowtail.

**25th October**

Italian pasta makers used to knead DOUGH with their BARE FEET.

**26th October**

The Eiffel Tower can be 15cm taller during the summer because of the heat.

**27th October**

Scientists estimate that the AVERAGE person can distinguish at least 1,000,000,000,000 (a TRILLION) different smells.

**28th October**

Earthworms have 5 hearts.

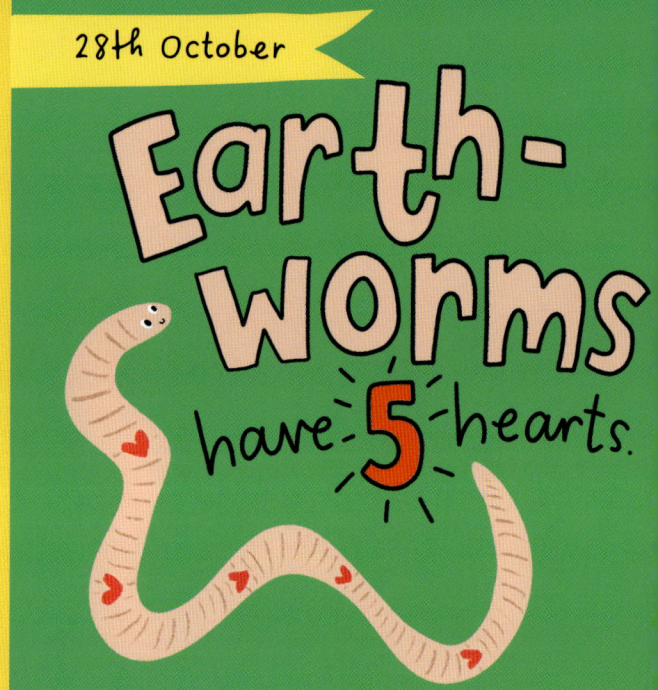

**29th October**

Dogs can LEARN the age, health and mood of other dogs by SNIFFING their bums.

**30th October**

A primary school in India asks parents to plant a TREE instead of paying TUITION.

31st October

A city in New Hampshire, USA, holds the RECORD for the most JACK-O'-LANTERNS on display, with 30,581 lit in the city.

### 2nd November

The tiny pocket in JEANS was ORIGINALLY made to hold a pocket watch.

### 3rd November

You can make your own STAMP at the Postal Museum in Bhutan.

### 4th November

A PIZZA delivery person once carried an order 16,950 kilometres from the UK to Australia to raise money for charity.

**5th November**

The **LARGEST**-EVER firework display consisted of 810,904 fireworks and lasted for 1 hour, 1 minute and 32.35 seconds.

**6th November**

In Taiwan it is polite to **BURP** after FINISHING your meal.

**7th November**

All Major League Baseball umpires have to wear BLACK underwear in case their trousers split.

**8th November**

Some birds, such as the **BLUE TIT**, often hang **UPSIDE DOWN** to eat.

**9th November**

A male **OSTRICH** can **ROAR** like a **LION**.

### 10th November

An 80-year-old JAPANESE man was the OLDEST person to climb MOUNT EVEREST, the HIGHEST mountain on Earth.

### 11th November

If you're right-handed, the FINGERNAILS on your LEFT hand GROW FASTER. The opposite is true if you're left-handed.

### 12th November

In TIBET people greet each other by STICKING out their TONGUES.

13th November

Taumatawhakatangihangakoauauotamateaturipukakapikimaungahoronukupokaiwhenuakitanatahu

There's a hill in New Zealand whose name has 85 letters. Not surprisingly, people just call it Taumata Hill.

## 14th November

# male bottlenose DOLPHINS

have NAMES for each other, which they call by using UNIQUE whistles.

DAVE!

## 15th November

Diamonds and PENCIL LEADS are made of the SAME material: GRAPHITE.

18th November

**Lopburi** in Thailand holds an ANNUAL MONKEY FESTIVAL, where monkeys are fed a BANQUET of FRUITS and VEGETABLES as a *thank you* for attracting tourists.

19th November

A GROUP of rhinoceroses is called a CRASH.

**20th November**

In Wisconsin, USA, there is a DOLL-MAKER who creates customized dolls for children with disabilities or INJURIES.

**21st November**

Hummingbirds are the ONLY birds that can fly BACKWARDS.

**22nd November**

It's IMPOSSIBLE for MOST people to LICK their own ELBOW.

### 23rd November

A TURKEY can BLUSH — when it is scared or EXCITED, the pale skin on its head and neck changes colour.

### 24th November

A Durian is a BIG spiky fruit that grows in Southeast Asia. It's so SMELLY that it is banned on public transport.

**25th November**

Surrounding yourself with **HAPPY PEOPLE** will make you HAPPIER.

**26th November**

Woolly mammoths could have **BLOND, BROWN** or **GINGER FUR.**

**27th November**

# BEES can fly HIGHER than MOUNT EVEREST.

**28th November**

Train stations in FRANCE and LONDON have installed vending machines that print SHORT STORIES.

**29th November**

There are **10 COUNTRIES** in the world where 97-100% of ELECTRICITY comes from RENEWABLE sources, HELPING save the planet.

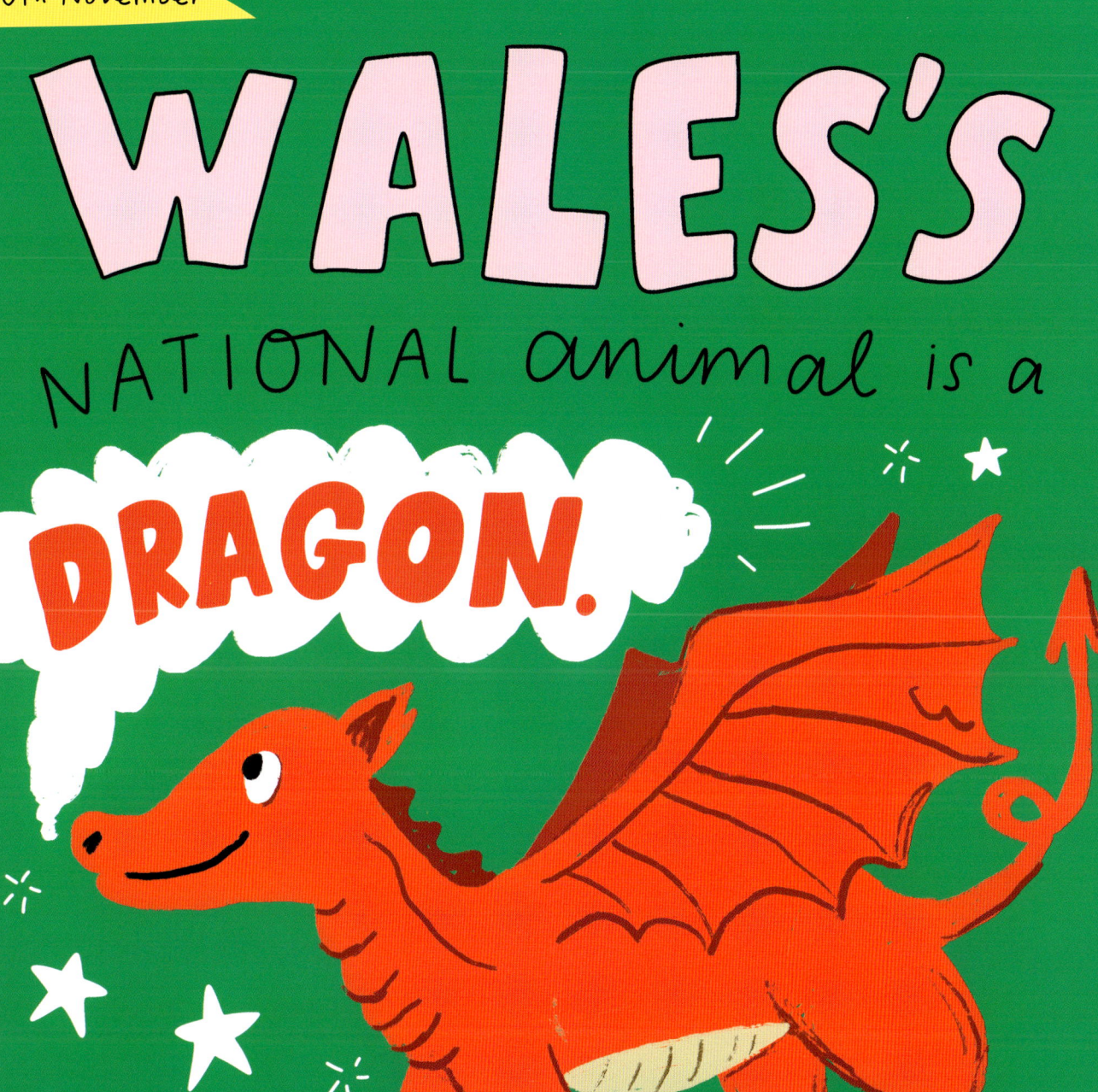

# December

**1st December**

Volunteers at an Indian elephant conservation centre knit jumpers to keep ELEPHANTS warm in near-freezing temperatures.

**2nd December**

Genetically, the children of two sets of IDENTICAL twins, although COUSINS, are more like SIBLINGS.

**3rd December**

The Miracle Berry is a fruit found across West Africa that can make LEMONS taste sweet.

**4th December**

Japanese pygmy seahorses are so TINY that HUNDREDS of them can fit in your hand.

**5th December**

The Italian town of Collecchio has a law that FIREWORK displays must be SILENT to avoid causing stress to PETS and WILDLIFE.

### 6th December

A pet HAMSTER can run up to 9 kilometres a NIGHT on a wheel.

### 7th December

A CUCAMELON is the size of a GRAPE but looks like a watermelon and tastes like cucumber.

### 8th December

The Amazon river is home to PINK DOLPHINS.

**9th December**

In Sweden, you can stay in an ice hotel - even the beds are made of ice and snow.

**10th December**

When you do a GOOD DEED your BRAIN releases feel-GOOD chemicals - so being kinder to others means you're also being kinder to yourself.

**11th December**

Our NOSE is a NATURAL lie detector; it gets WARMER if we tell a fib!

**12th December**

GRASSHOPPERS have EARS on their knees.

**13th December**

EVERY STEP you take uses 200 DIFFERENT MUSCLES in the BODY.

**15th December**

During certain months Colombia's Caño Cristales river turns into a **LIQUID RAINBOW** of red, blue, yellow, orange and green.

**16th December**

**Norway** once knighted a **PENGUIN.**

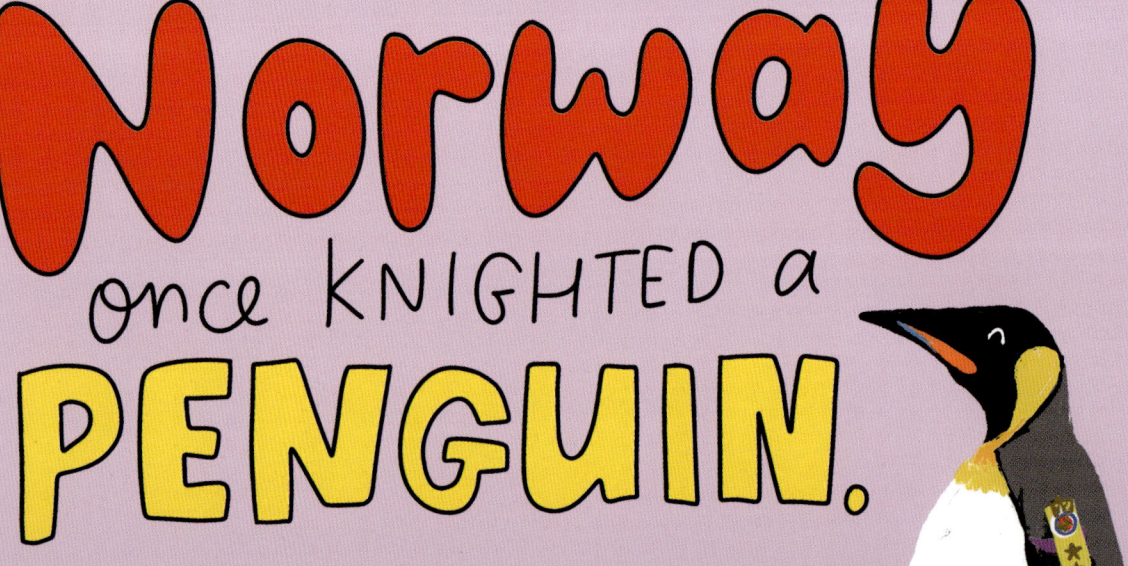

## 20th December

On the MOON SKIPPING is faster than WALKING.

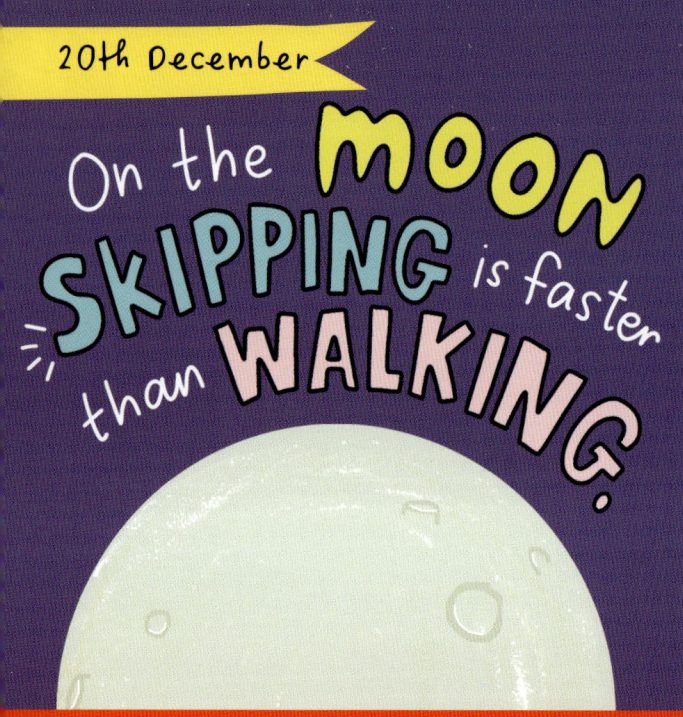

## 21st December

In 17th-century Japan people put CHILLIES in their socks to keep their toes WARM.

## 22nd December

A jiffy is a REAL unit of TIME.

in a jiffy!

## 23rd December

The LARGEST CHOIR in the world consisted of a whopping 121,440 people.

24th December

# Jolabokaflod,

or Christmas book flood, is the Icelandic TRADITION of gifting BOOKS at Christmas time so the nights can be spent reading and drinking hot chocolate.

25th December

"JINGLE BELLS" was the first song played in SPACE, when it was broadcast on a space flight in 1965.

**26th December**

A **Pianist** named Paul Barton, who used to perform to THOUSANDS, now plays the piano to SOOTHE injured and blind ELEPHANTS.

**27th December**

**Looking at trees** can help reduce stress and INCREASE focus.

**28th December**

In Berlin unsold Christmas trees are used as SNACKS for ZOO ELEPHANTS.

**29th December**

A glow-worm's GLOW can be seen from up to 50 metres away.

**30th December**

There are 31,536,000 SECONDS in a year.

31st December

The confetti that falls on **New York's** TIMES SQUARE at MIDNIGHT on New Year's Eve is literally made of DREAMS & WISHES. People send in their HOPES for the NEW year, and these are included in the CONFETTI.